SU

Where Do W   ...... Here

Chaos or Community?

ABBEY BEATHAN

Text Copyright © ABBEY BEATHAN

All rights reserved. No part of this guide may be reproduced in any form without permission in writing from the publisher except in the case of brief quotations embodied in critical articles or reviews.

Legal & Disclaimer

The information contained in this book is not designed to replace or take the place of any form of medicine or professional medical advice. The information in this book has been provided for educational and entertainment purposes only.

The information contained in this book has been compiled from sources deemed reliable, and it is accurate to the best of the Author's knowledge; however, the Author cannot guarantee its accuracy and validity and cannot be held liable for any errors or omissions. Changes are periodically made to this book. You must consult your doctor or get professional medical advice before using any of the suggested remedies, techniques, or information in this book. Images used in this book are not the same as of that of the actual book. This is a totally separate and different entity from that of the original book titled: "Where Do We Go From Here"

Upon using the information contained in this book, you agree to hold harmless the Author from and against any damages, costs, and expenses, including any legal fees potentially resulting from the application of any of the information provided by this guide. This disclaimer applies to any damages or injury caused by the use and application, whether directly or indirectly, of any advice or information presented, whether for breach of contract, tort, negligence, personal injury, criminal intent, or under any other cause of action.

You agree to accept all risks of using the information presented inside this book. You need to consult a professional medical practitioner in order to ensure you are both able and healthy enough to participate in this program.

Table of Contents

The Book at a Glance vi

Introduction.. 1

Foreword 5

Chapter 1: Where Are We?... 9

Chapter 2: Black Power.. 14

Chapter 3: Racism and the White Backlash 19

Chapter 4: The Dilemma of Negro Americans 24

Chapter 5: Where We Are Going 29

Chapter 6: The World House 35

Appendix: Programs and Prospects............................ 39

    Education 39

    Employment... 40

    Rights.. 41

    Housing 42

Conclusion.. 43

Final Thoughts.. 48

The Book at a Glance

It is no secret that Martin Luther King, Jr. was one of the finest men that lived in this world. Because of him, and the black men during his time, the civil, voting, and open housing rights movement became a reality. Thanks to his efforts, the segregation between whites and blacks was abolished.

During his lifetime, he served as a Baptist minister and leader of the Southern Christian Leadership Conference (SCLC). He championed the nonviolence and civil obedience methods in the movements he led, which yielded effective results.

Aside from fighting for the Negroes, he also sided with the poor and challenged the government to create social reforms. Because of those, he was accused of cooperating and being influenced by socialists and communist nations.

The FBI was in constant surveillance of him. Even the NSA moved behind the scenes to watch him. However, no substantial evidence was found to incriminate him for the alleged collusion. Nonetheless, government entities found something else: He was a womanizer and adulterer. This part of his life was later revealed to the public. However, his close allies and even his family knew about his womanizing ways.

It was unfortunate that King died young. He was assassinated in the hotel where he was staying with his close allies. A gunshot killed him, and the one who killed him, James Earl

Ray, was immediately captured and sentenced.

Due to his positive impact on the country and the way he achieved his goals, he was given a Nobel Peace Prize in 1964. In 1971, Martin Luther King Day was celebrated as a holiday in multiple cities and states to honor his birthday. In 1986, it officially became a US Federal Holiday.

At this point, you already know the most important things about the author of this book. Do note that this copy is a summarized and compacted version of the book. Due to the size and richness of the book in factual information and important anecdotes, it is advised that you read the book in its entirety.

On the other hand, the compression of the book into this summarized version can easily make it prone to misinterpretation. At present, the topics discussed in this literature are still sensitive issues and can easily offend some people.

Moving forward, King has focused on two things in this book: the black civil rights movement and the abolishment of poverty. He shares the story from his point of view of the marches he led and the voice of the people involved in the march.

In addition, he provides commentary on the issues they were tackling. He usually started with diagnosing the problem, then stating proof of the existence of the problem, and discussing the current actions done by the people who were involved and responsible. And lastly, he provided an opinion on what is the best course of action to solve the problem.

As a side note, the book can be considered long and boring for the modern reader. It contains long passages of paragraphs and one can easily get lost in its content. But despite that, it is crucial that you read this book from cover to cover. It will give you valuable insights on how it is to be oppressed and to achieve freedom from such oppression.

Here are the chapter-by-chapter reviews at a glance:

- Introduction: Vincent Harding was requested to provide an introduction to this book by its publisher. He mostly talked about his experiences with King, and the things they frequently talked and discussed.

- Foreword: The foreword, on the other hand, was written by King's wife, Coretta Scott King. She provided an additional introduction for the book and a brief overview of King's life and achievements.

- Chapter 1: Where Are We? Here, King established who the blacks were. He wrote about their sufferings and small victories over their oppressors. The chapter included many excerpts of the success of the nonviolent marches and demonstrations that he personally started and attended.

The chapter is full of anecdotes of what happened during the marches. Reading his words, you will feel as if he were personally guiding you in the jam-packed crowd that protested for equality in the 1960s. You will also gain an idea about the key players in the movement and the people's sentiments.

- Chapter 2: Black Power. Despite the success of the demonstrations and rallies that King organized, there were still some ups and downs in his and the movement's journey — particularly, the creation and usage of the slogan, "black power."

  King discussed why it was a bad idea to use the words "black power" in their movement. He believed that it failed because of the misrepresentation of their goals and cause. He also talked about the negative emotions and reactions of the blacks toward the white folks that were helping their cause.

- Chapter 3: Racism and The White Backlash. This chapter is about the delusion of the American white people. They believe that they are not racists or prejudiced against people of color. However, it was just an unconscious façade. Even if they wanted to be not that "guy," their behavior and knee-jerk reactions when talked about having Negroes in their lives clearly showed that they were just faking it to look good.

Aside from that, King lashed out at religion, faith, and the church for supporting the act of slavery in the nation. He claimed that the church needed to rectify their past actions and work on helping the blacks regain their position in the world as human beings.

King also referred to the roots of racism and slavery in the world. He talked about about how pseudoscience had exacerbated the problems with slavery, and how America treated the blacks as if they were things or just property that can be used.

- Chapter 4: The Dilemma of Negro Americans. The fight that they were fighting for was crucial for the advancement of the nation as a whole. However, they were already weary of the constant resistance they encountered and the traumas they experienced. And these concerns made blacks turn to negative habits and even addiction just to be able to cope.

King analyzed this behavior, and was able to come up with the proper solutions and suggestions to correct such issues. These solutions, if followed, would also help in strengthening the movement for freedom and civil rights.

- Chapter 5: Where Are We Going? King urged people to ask where they are. Once that is answered, the next question will be, "Where are we going?" This chapter goes into detail about the current actions of the government toward the protests that the blacks have continued to do — even after achieving great results.

  The chapter discusses the next actions that the Negroes needed to take to maintain the progress in society when it comes to treating people of color. On the other hand, this is the part where King started to tackle poverty.

- Chapter 6: The World House. Here, King talked about the international scene of poverty and tolerance. He focused on letting the blacks know that they are not the only ones suffering in the world. Despite receiving the most hardships, they must know that they are not alone and they should always lend a helping hand to those who are also oppressed. On the other hand, King urged nations, especially the wealthy ones, to help in eradicating poverty and segregation in the world. When it came to individuals, he encouraged them to stay away from materialism, and instead focus on societal concerns and freedom revolutions.

He also advised the United States to lead the revolution of values. After all, despite being a young country, the United States had already amassed wealth and leverage on a global scale, which made it the most powerful and influential country in the world.

- Appendix: Programs and Prospects. In this part of the book, King tackled and discussed four important elements that Negroes and impoverished people should have: education, employment, rights, and housing.

Each section is full of accurate analysis and suggestions on how to resolve the turmoil plaguing each of the basic needs. He also provided a brief overview on the situation of those sectors during his time.

Introduction

Vincent Harding wrote the introductory part of this book. He used the introduction to let readers know his and King's shared sentiments and friendship. Mostly, he said that most of the book focused on questions and answers that he had heard from the people he had the chance to be with.

Harding was a longtime friend of King. He was there for King during the last decade of his life. He was asked to write the introduction for this book by its publisher, Beacon Press. And as he wrote this part, memories of their times together flooded him with nostalgia and other emotions.

King had a way with words, and every story he told compelled his listeners. He could have solely written books to spread the teachings and ideas he had, but he chose a much more direct approach: Come to the protests himself.

And as his journey took him to lots of places and allowed him to meet wonderful people, he was able to realize the most important things in life. "Where are we?" is a question most people ask themselves. It is a question that probes the self. It is a question that Americans need to ask themselves.

By answering this question, King has led people to march

nonviolently in the most racist states. And in 1965, one of the fruits of the movement bore fruit: The president signed the Voting Rights Act. It was a way to relieve the blacks from the oppression they had experienced for so long.

People should always take the time to reflect on their actions and deeds. They need to examine themselves. This was how King found his motivation to join the rally for the achievement of social rights and freedom. And he immediately found success in his movement.

When President Lyndon B. Johnson signed the Voting Rights Act in 1965, people knew and understood that King was able to come up with the best approach in tackling social issues as grave as segregation and racism. At the same time, he was inspired to work on this book.

Before the movement, the groups that led the marches had encountered some troubles. One of the biggest was financing. Since most people joining the cause were stricken with poverty, they needed to uplift themselves first before they could even move for others.

Something was truly wrong with the economic system of America. Despite the first few groups who tried to change the societal, economical, and political situation of the American blacks, poverty and racism were still rampant. The only thing that the poor had was an abundance of compassion and empathy. It would be ideal if the government was able to come up with a way to distribute the wealth of the nation, especially to those who needed it the most.

Anyway, the book will give you a glimpse of the hardships of the blacks and how King, together with his people, struggled to gain the justice that they deserved. It will also give you a glimpse — practically a firsthand experience on how terrible racism has become in America.

The organizers and members of the movement were the ones who inspired King to write this book. But he did not stop here. He gave his all to bring the best out of the Negro community. Despite the anger and hatred, he was able to make them abide by the law and protest peacefully.

There were times that things got out of hand, and the resistance against the marches caused injuries in a few of the movement's brothers. Some even died during the protest. But in spite of those, they were resolute and determined to carry out the movement, and continued revolutionizing their world with the absence of violence.

King also knew that to be successful, the movement needed the help of the whites. He was right. Yet the people who were on King's side knew that it would be difficult to pull off. The members of the community, after all, already had built up enough angst against the colorless.

He was truly the Mahatma Gandhi of the black people. He identified with his members. He knew how they felt and what they were going through and empathized with them. They were underprivileged, but he made sure that they would not be in that state for long. Vincent even asserted that King paved the way for Barack Obama and it would have been truly wonderful if the two had met.

In this book, you will also see all the facets of Martin Luther King, Jr.: a minister, a political analyst, a regular citizen, and a family man. He was truly a man with a mission. And despite his love for the black people, he was not scared to talk against and reprimand them from time to time.

At the end of it all, King just wanted a country with an integrated and loving community, free from color prejudice. He did not want America to have fake "integration." He did not want to stay with the chaotic segregation full of hypocrisy.

Foreword

This section was written by Martin Luther King Jr.'s wife, Coretta Scott King. She said that her husband acted as the front-runner of the revolution and had been planning to write this book ever since the movement started.

In his book, King focused on looking for the roots of discord that existed in the nation — racism to be precise. It took a year before the National Advisory Commission on Civil Disorders would act on the things written on this book.

Aside from that, he focused on poverty. King emphasized how the international scene needed to look and act on it. He wholeheartedly defended them in this book, and he even proposed solutions on how to abolish poverty completely.

Overall, this book embodies everything that King was and all the things he fought for. The solutions he proposed would save the country and the world from self-destructing. And even after his death, the world had to do something to achieve the social and economic justice he sacrificed all his life for.

During the time it was written, the book served as the manifesto for the blacks and poor people. King was truly bold. He did not back down from any person or party. It did not matter if you were white, black, poor, or rich. As long as there was something wrong in your ways, King would point it out.

Of course, the book provided empowerment to the Negroes. But it did not mean that they were perfect in King's eyes. He acknowledged that they were scarred and flawed, and thus needed someone to guide them. And there he was: He served as the champion of the masses and the oppressed.

It was unfortunate that he met his end at a young age. He would have served more people in dire need of a revolution: a revolution of values. He would have defended the poor, and pushed the government and other countries to destroy poverty once and for all.

The timing of the republication of the book was impeccable. In 2010, the first black president of the United States had been in power for a year already. Half a decade ago, blacks did not even have the opportunity to seek employment. Now, not only did black people "almost" have equal job opportunities as whites, but a black man was also able to get the highest government position in the country.

King once predicted that the progress of civil rights would be downright slow and would always be in danger of stagnating.

He was right. Despite his death and people living and continuing his legacy, racism is still prominent until today. Thankfully, segregation has been fully abolished in the country.

On the other hand, some countries have heeded his call. They are now fighting poverty and have become tolerable and accepting of other races and countries. Yes, the world is still far from perfect. In many parts of the world, especially in the Middle East, hints of racial tolerance are still non-existent.

Many of the countries living near the arid desert of the Sahara are still fighting against each other. Religious and extremist terrorists are still hunting down potential victims. At this point, King's concept of a harmonious world is still hidden in the far future.

Despite being written half a century ago, King's message to the people is still relevant. For blacks, it is a good history book. It will always remind them of what their parents and grandparents did and sacrificed for them to live in a freer world, almost free from persecution and oppression.

For whites, the book serves as a lesson. God did make humans in His image, but the Bible never said that he made them after his skin color. The lesson here is that the attempt to rationalize evil is far more sinister than the evil being defended.

Also, everyone should always remember that privileges come with a price. Even though the white folks of the 20th century were truly fortunate to have the government and society on their side, poverty still took control of most of them.

For the politically correct police and online justice keyboard warriors, the book serves as a reminder that words alone cannot help the oppressed and victims of injustice. If they are truly defenders of the fraught, they should go out, act, and actually help.

For the oppressed, this book is for you to read. It does not matter what kind of oppression you are feeling. Racism is not the only thing that could tyrannize people. You will surely be motivated and inspired by King's words.

Chapter 1: Where Are We?

President Lyndon Johnson signed the historic Voting Rights Act on August 6, 1965. The violent reaction of sheriffs toward the nonviolent voting rights demonstration in Selma, Alabama only hastened its legislation. Despite the enactment of the act, it was clear that the treatment toward black Americans was still evidently poor, especially in the Southern states.

Negroes were not the only victims of violent hate crimes. The resistance against the marches in the South murdered both white and black civil rights workers even after the president had signed the bill. This sparked violent reprisals from young Negroes. And because of that, the civil rights movement gradually weakened and disappeared from media coverage. Sympathy toward the "oppressed" dwindled into nothingness.

Due to this, the civil rights movement got stuck in phase one. And instead of giving Negroes equal rights, the white folks only gave the blacks civility and decency. Previous white allies left the movement. Phase two, which should have been the movement to acquire equality, never materialized for a long time.

CHAPTER 1

—O—

Americans believe that they support Negroes. But they do nothing to make equality a reality. They wait until the next Selma or Birmingham to happen before they act again and step up. It was a complete contradiction. They say they wanted change to happen, but they still stuck with the status quo.

The attempts to further improve the treatment of black Americans yielded results that were far from significant. It did not cost much to push this change. Letting the Negroes have lunch or do activities with fellow white Americans would not burn any tax money. There are no consequences in abolishing segregation. In short, the coexistence of blacks and whites isn't that much of a hardship after all.

Aside from the issue of skin color, the country was wracked with problems regarding ignorance and poverty. And even though tackling and resolving those issues came with a hefty price tag, one has to consider it a good investment that would have rewarding returns.

Negroes at that point in time received half the good and twice the bad. Whites considered blacks as half a person. They received half the amount of pay. Segregated schools for black children received half the funding. Almost three out of four black workers only got menial jobs.

There were twice as more Negroes than whites drafted in recent wars. The war killed twice of the number of blacks than whites in action — that fact was not a secret.

You do not even need to know the numbers to know the sheer unfairness that Negroes had to go through in life. Discrimination was — and still is — rampant. Whites have a problem with having a black neighbor, friend, or most especially, lover.

The commitment to change was too shallow. The ones who were involved with the protests and the passing of the Voting Rights Act were the exception.

Observers have commented that if change happens in one go, the recipients, the Negroes, were not prepared for it. Just imagine how prepared other Americans are.

Despite not attaining the change they wanted, the Negroes strived to make it happen. They did more work. They wanted to be more educated. In contrast, whites were not doing anything. They failed to exert even the smallest effort to educate themselves about racial equality and tolerance.

The movement was able to achieve phase one of its goal. However, implementation became a problem. Even if the

CHAPTER 1

government mandated school desegregation, only 10% of the nation's schools complied. Given this situation, it became obvious that with every step that blacks made, whites would always stop them and consider them to have gone too far.

This has shown that while Americans hate injustice, they are unwilling to do something to change that.

— O —

The nonstop hindrances of whites to the movement discouraged the blacks. But they forgot one important thing: Progress is not linear. Obstacles and challenges will always appear. And people need small victories to achieve success.

The stagnation of any effort to obtain full freedom has become apparent. The Negroes never progressed much in changing the way the world treated them before the movement. However, after the marches, these same people felt that there was hope. The stagnation dissipated and energy and encouragement started to flow again.

More establishments opened for Negroes in the South, which was a feat. After all, the South was the stronghold — or capital if you want to call it that way — of racism.

—O—

Around 1967, Negroes became the instigators of change and not just the beneficiaries of it. The Negro revolution continued. The movement on the North was partially successful. The South, on the other hand, appeared to be impregnable despite their efforts.

Even though the rising awareness and activities within the black society had become apparent, the number of Negroes actively participating in the war to obtain freedom and equality was relatively small. Another potential concern was the optimism that they displayed. The blacks thought that a small cost would be enough to achieve change. They were wrong.

This consequently led to nonviolent protests turning ugly. Rage consumed the demonstrators. And it made whites fear possible riots. This created another divide and encouraged fascism. Blacks became the villains.

At the end of the day, the events that transpired and the behavior displayed by both sides revealed that if the two oppositions worked together, the much-needed change would have happened faster.

Chapter 2: Black Power

In June 1966, a bullet wounded James Meredith. He led the Freedom March in Mississippi. The news reported that he died, but the opposite was true — Meredith was able to recover. Luther, together with his staff, visited him in the hospital. He tried to persuade Meredith to march with them, but the latter declined.

CORE (Congress of Racial Equality), SNCC (Student Nonviolent Coordinating Committee), and SCLC (Southern Christian Leadership Conference) sponsored the march. They started the march in Highway 51, where Meredith's incident took place.

During the march, several heated debates arose. Some felt that they did not want to take the nonviolent path anymore. Some decided that the march should have been limited to just black people only — to the point they wanted to change the song "We Shall Overcome" to "We Shall Overrun."

Luther concluded that bitterness caused the negative sentiments he heard. The night after, Luther decided to air out his thoughts about maintaining the nonviolent stance and the morality and importance of making the march interracial.

After that, the group was able to achieve a temporary agreement. It did not stop the negative talks, though. Fortunately, the enthusiasm of the participants, new and old, pushed the negative topics far to the background.

The march reached Greenwood. The movement grew larger. At its center was the slogan, "Black Power." Before, the additional members of the movement had trickled in like raindrops during a brief squall. Now, they were raining down hard as if there was a storm.

Luther felt that the slogan was a poor choice of words. The word "black" excluded the white people who joined the movement; while the word "power" sounded violent.

He expressed this concern to other high-ranking movement officials. They countered Luther's sentiments, but they were convinced about the reasons he presented to them. In the end, the slogan died, but the media clung to it.

People perceived the slogan "Black Power" in varying ways. Some of the interpretation came out good; some were offensive. But what was important was what it represented.

It was a cry caused by disappointments — with all the brutalities that have happened, the failure to fulfill promises, and the never-ending hardships aggravated further by white folks. It did not just come out of nowhere. It was a cry that stemmed from continual oppression and discrimination. It was in direct opposition of white power.

Aside from being a cry for revolution, it was a call for people to rise and achieve their goals. Power does not equate to violence. In the slogan, power referred to the ability to reach ambitions. The Negroes did not have that kind of power. The whites did.

"Black Power" was also a demand for blacks to man up. For the past few decades, Negroes grew up believing that they were inferior compared to other races. This has been a direct result of slavery and the disregard of the contributions of blacks in history and the country itself.

Despite the positive merits that Black Power represented, negativity tainted it. It heavily portrayed blacks as the eternal underdogs and whites as the evil oppressors. And it did not help that Negroes lost hope and turned to anger and rage instead. Those factors made the movement weak.

The problem of losing hope was that it diminished the flame that kept the movement going. It started from despair, and people can only go so far with despair fueling the movement. And as a cry of disappointment, Black Power sans hope only bred a continuous stream of negative emotions and thinking: fatalism and self-pity.

Another rising concern about the Black Power movement was that it was reverse racism, which was stressed before. Black people were the good guys; white people were the baddies. It was self-defeating. It was an irony: The Black Power movement combated isolation and segregation by applying isolation and segregation.

That was not the movement's goal. Yet the members of the black community started to think like that. As Luther suggested, it would not work that way. For the movement to work, it was crucial that they work together with other races.

Plus, the biggest issue with Black Power was the tendency of its members to resort to violence. Anybody in the movement could have put a stop to it — after all, most of the time, violence was to retaliate or to perform self-defense. It was a healthy reaction from people who were repressed and oppressed.

But a movement based on self-defense and retaliation would easily crumble. After all, aggressive and self-defensive violence are still forms of violence.

CHAPTER 2

Movements with violence at their core never triumph. True, there were cases that it could be a good means to reach an expected end. However, those instances were the exception. They were movements done by a small minority with the backing of a majority.

Violence and hatred only result to fear and terror — not to mention that they also instigate confusion and guilt. And if the movement chose to go down that path, nobody would be able to count the number of dead bodies that would end up on the streets. What's more, the probability of them succeeding with the revolution would dwindle down to zero.

Chapter 3: Racism and the White Backlash

The main reason that white people have oppressed the Negroes and degraded their status lower than dirt was not because they were inferior, but because white folks believed that they were superior. America has a schizophrenic personality when it comes to race — a duality of love and hate. Americans love democracy but impose tyranny toward the Negroes. It made the country move a step forward and a step backward. King referred to this phenomenon as the white backlash.

Racism is deep-rooted in Americans. It was an ideological justification that became faith. It became an excuse to allow white folks to increase their economic and political power through the slavery of blacks. And as it progressed, the idea of one's race being superior spread and strengthened.

Racism was the spark that started the Nazi movement. The Nazis believed that inferior races should sacrifice themselves for Nazis and other races that they considered superior and pure. This might not be the same kind of racism practiced in America, but it was relatively similar, with the only difference of white folks using segregation and deprivation instead of elimination.

CHAPTER 3

Despite the fact that the foundation of America had sprung up from democracy and opposition to monarchy, the founders and first people just ignored and tolerated slavery. Before and after the Declaration of Independence, European monarchies, merchants, and nobles traded Negroes as goods. America was the biggest importer while Great Britain was the largest supplier.

In the New World, people treated slaves as property. Pseudoscience declared that blacks were inferior. The Bible and religion protected and justified the idea of slavery. God created humans according to His image. God was not black; hence Negroes were not considered men. With those things becoming rampant in the world, white folks perfectly and swiftly rationalized slavery in everyone's minds.

Most — if not all — of America's Founding Fathers were slaveowners. Some of them, even though they themselves owned slaves, questioned slavery. However, most of them were unable to air their sentiments about the Negroes in public.

Even Abraham Lincoln, known for his Emancipation Proclamation, had gone through a similar experience. It was during the Civil War that he needed to face this conundrum. It was true that slavery was the main cause of the war, but he did not want to turn against his "people." Despite his constituents and close allies pressuring him, it took some time before Lincoln finally relented and did it: freeing the slaves.

Unfortunately, freeing the slaves was only the start of the solution. It was far from the end. Previous slaves had no property and no means to live. While the government gave white peasants land and allowed them to settle for free, it denied blacks those same privileges.

America's commitment to equality has deluded its people. You can compare America's situation to the prodigal son depicted in the Bible. As of now, it has strayed — gone down the path of racism. And its people are waiting for it to come home to its roots.

America focused on power, wealth, and size. It abandoned developing a just society. It focused more on sending men to the moon, where no human or constituent lives, than taking care of its suffering inhabitants.

The white liberal was privileged to have a voice in the civil rights movement, the government, the welfare agencies, and the church. These liberals were the biggest hindrances of the movement. Some supported the movement, but they still needed to let go of their biases and prejudice in order to become truly liberal.

Even though they were a minority, some black members of the movement degraded the purity of the cause. Racism crept up on them and they started to harbor ill feelings toward Semites and whites. That only goes to show that racism is a disease that the American people must eradicate in their lives.

Most of the black members, however, felt that they needed to have full control of the movement. For the first few years, white liberals had been the ones at the top — and they did a good job. Now, since the events after multiple successes of the march empowered blacks, it was time for the liberal whites to gracefully pass the baton to the Negroes.

The church has a responsibility to support the movement. For the past few decades, it was the main culprit behind spreading the word that slavery was morally right. The church, together with the movement, must take a stand and cleanse the world of slavery and segregation.

Finally, it is up to the men to finish what the movement

started. The abolishment of segregation does not end with the creation of laws. It must be adhered to.

Naturally, white folks should not ignore the problem of blacks. Both are part of society after all. And in this sense, with the white folks having greater power and influence, the key to the Negroes' freedom lies in the white men's hands, literally and figuratively.

White Americans should commit themselves to helping their colored brothers and sisters. They should not just pity them, but they should empathize and act. Pity is just a feeling, an inactive action that lets them be sorry for the blacks without doing anything. Empathy is a feeling that lets them be sorry *with* the blacks. There is a huge difference, and the latter will make it easier for change to happen.

Chapter 4: The Dilemma of Negro Americans

The main dilemma of Negro Americans is symbiotic to the dilemma of white Americans. The schizophrenic back-and-forth of whites — their ambivalence toward blacks — stemmed from their position as the oppressor of blacks. In the same vein, Negroes found themselves in this situation due to their position of being the oppressed. And it is impossible for whites to understand everything completely, especially the oppression the blacks received from them for centuries.

Negroes and their suffering are one of a kind. They are not like immigrants. They are not like traditional slaves. Other races, particularly white ones, did not treat blacks like human beings.

The Emancipation Proclamation liberated the Negroes in 1863. However, the proclamation was not able to broker peace among the people and slaveowners in the South. The two sides in the Civil war fought for the blacks, but they never had a place to run for safety and the majority of blacks became slaves again after the war was over.

Freed slaves were able to stabilize their lives, but black women gained an advantage due to their frequent exposure to educated white children. Black men only knew hard labor. Finding employment proved almost impossible. Expressing their frustration to the public led to persecution. Expressing their frustration in private led to beaten wives and kids.

The Negroes lived in ghettos. The American people forgot and ignored them for a long time. The blacks were voiceless and they wanted people to notice them. They desired it so much that the most of the leaders of the movement considered the demonstration that led to a riot, which resulted to the deaths of 34 blacks, an accomplishment. From their point of view, it was a success because the people noticed them.

Rising from the ghetto was an extreme challenge for the Negroes. Businessmen charged them more for rent, utility, and other basic needs — the bane of the "color tax." If they got a loan, they were saddled with high interest rates because they were considered "credit risks." When they got a job, they got reduced pay.

Open housing could have been the perfect ticket for the Negroes, but the ones in charge of the housing projects blatantly denied them access. It did not matter if you were of high intellect or position; if you were black, you cannot get a home.

Whites were offended by the situation, too. After all, they said they were not racist. But when asked about having blacks in their neighborhood, they generated opposing statements, which all led to one conclusion: Blacks were not welcome in their neighborhood. This was a modern take on black slavery.

—O—

This dilemma has led blacks to resort to negative means of coping. These negative means will cause the blacks to self-destruct. And if they do not do anything about it quick, all will be for naught.

Primarily, the biggest issue is passivity. Blacks should remember that everything can be achieve through action. Nothing will happen or will change through inaction. Also, antisocialism, gang warfare, delinquency, and addiction will only make matters worse.

King listed these steps to solve the dilemma:

1. Generate self-worth: The experiences of getting enslaved and being oppressed had diminished the self-worth of Negroes. It made them ashamed of themselves. However, if they truly want to be free of

such treatment, they should start believing in themselves and be proud of who and what they are.

2. Unite as a group: Negroes have become distrustful even toward his own kind. If they want to get past that or make changes in the society, it is crucial for them to unite and move as one. They may not agree on all things, and that's okay — they don't need to. They just need to unite for a common goal, which is to alleviate their life full of oppression and suppression.

3. Take advantage of your freedom: At this point, the Negroes are already free. They are not slaves anymore. It is true that white folks are still avoiding and segregating them, but they can do something about it. There is no reason to hide anymore.

4. Create plans and programs: Time heals wounds, but there are things that it cannot mend: one of those is oppression. If the previous statement were false, slavery would have ended centuries ago. Because of that, Negroes should not just stand idly by and wait; they must devise a plan and act on it.

5. The middle class should join the fight: Despite the intense measures white folks have placed to subdue blacks, a few of them were able to swim out of the swamp. And even if they were already out of the

ghettos, they should not just watch and assume that they are not involved anymore. All blacks need them, and if they work together with the movement, they will all benefit.

6. Help the society outside the movement: The blacks should never forget to help other races or victims of oppression. They are not the only one deserving to be saved; the civil rights movement is not exclusively for them. They should remember that the movement is for all of the oppressed.

Chapter 5: Where We Are Going

The government has expressed interest in civil rights, but so far it has done nothing concrete. The government claimed that it had written programs and plans. But the black people did not need those; what they needed was action.

The solution was to amass strength to push the government into doing something. Because of that, King and other black organizations formed and carried out the nonviolent marches. However, they were not perfect. Often, they led to failure.

Blacks must admit that they are not yet capable of developing power in the country. The marches were a success in that they took the movement closer to its goal. But as mentioned, they were not perfect — everything was impromptu and done haphazardly. So even though they were effective, one cannot deny that the people involved were inexperienced.

But that was only natural. One person or a group cannot have all the answers in the world. And given that blacks were born and raised to be docile, to believe that they are nonexperts when it comes to political undertakings, and to think that they have nothing of significance to offer to the world.

CHAPTER 5

With so much baggage from their past, it is difficult for them to seek and assume a leadership position. Even within their own families, black men find it difficult to take charge.

It is a challenge for blacks to make themselves heard. With limited access to media, the most accessible, no, the *only* way was to let Americans hear them on the streets. And by asking blacks to stay off the streets, white Americans were, in effect, telling the Negroes to silence themselves and to stop standing up for their rights.

—O—

Thankfully, there are still some means for blacks to move and act for the sake of the cause. One of them was exerting influence in the committee. Just simply making friends with other blacks and nonblack people can allow the movement to have more supporters.

Even if those people would not personally come to the marches or donate anything, the moral support that they provide would be enough to motivate the Negroes to march on the street. Word of mouth can also be helpful. Establishing connections and getting sympathizers would raise awareness of the fight against discrimination and poverty.

Negroes can assert influence as a consumer and as an employee. Private sectors have employed more than two million Negroes — they comprise 20% of the workforce and 10% of the general population.

Negroes needed to band together and have proper representation in the workplace. One way was to join unions or create them.

Boycotting businesses and banks was a powerful tool to spread influence. It worked this way: If a business does not hire Negroes but does business with Negroes, boycotting that business will hurt its bottomline profit. Simply put, if the business does not start hiring Negroes, it will never have a Negro customer.

If the boycott was able to capture the interest of the business owner, allow negotiation to take place. If the negotiations did not go well, then there will be a full boycott with an additional public demonstration.

King, along with the African-American civil rights organization Southern Christian Leadership Conference (SCLC), established Operation Breadbasket. Its primary purpose was to secure better jobs for blacks by means of boycotts.

CHAPTER 5

Here's how it works: Boycotting starts with a simple negotiation by a black priest or minister. If the business owner turns down the clergyman's request or refuses to even consider a compromise, the latter will spread the word of boycotting the business through his congregation. And more often than not, the minister will also involve other clergymen in the area.

This tactic was effective because most businesses that catered to blacks often have no other customers except blacks. After all, these businesses were usually near ghettos and it is rare for white customers to set foot there. So, boycotting a business near a ghetto was almost always a guaranteed success.

In addition, people came to believe that if blacks say boycott, they mean business. In 1955, the Montgomery Bus Boycott happened because of the arrest of Rosa Parks. She refused to give up her seat to white passengers when their side of the bus was already full. She was arrested and fined for the incident.

It sparked the boycott, and at the same time, King rose to prominence. The city buses in Montgomery, Alabama instantly lost more than 40,000 black commuters.

Aside from the possible employment opportunities that

boycotting might bring, it could help them alleviate the "color tax." Usually, establishments that have black customers raise their prices to around 10% to 20%.

With lower pay, higher mortgage, and high interest rates from banks, black people in the ghettos often end up using all their money. And this prevents them from being able to save up.

—O—

Negroes have little chance to get a seat in the government. Their advantage, however, was numbers in the workforce. They can start influencing other people they are in contact with. And thanks to the labor movement and unions, Negroes have gained traction when it comes to connections.

However, voting had been a major problem with Negroes. They were disorganized. They did not want to dabble in politics. They had no political allies. And most candidates were white or picked by whites.

Those problems made it more difficult for black politicians to rise in power. Their supposed supporters did not want to get involved, and it will be almost impossible to form a base from the white community. So, they often start without any political alliances.

Negroes often found themselves veering away from politics because of multiple reasons. One, politicians, especially white ones, always manipulated blacks to garner more votes. Two, they were not optimistic about obtaining a seat in government. Three, they believed that it was better to focus on their own families instead of relying on the government.

—O—

Militant morale and radical reform are dangerous and hazardous. The good thing about the movement is that Negroes are cohesive. But at the same time, Negroes can be competitive and intolerant. They can easily become distrustful and unconfident.

—O—

Poverty remains one of the greatest issues of the nation. Interestingly, poor whites were twice as many than blacks. There are many established reasons for poverty: lack of education, few job opportunities, and poor housing. But according to King, the main culprit was the absence of guaranteed income.

The government must tie guaranteed income with median income. It must also be dynamic and level with the total social income. With those two, guaranteed income can abolish poverty. This does not only benefit blacks, but it will also benefit the poor, which is more than 65% white.

Chapter 6: The World House

The world house is a place where separated family members (races to be precise) live together — basically, it is the world. Advancements in technology have knitted together faraway separated countries.

Unfortunately, blacks are not welcome in the world house.

As with the progression of the sciences, social development must keep up. People of the world should not allow oppression to remain. Unfortunately, most people stubbornly cling to the status quo. In the West, this is a huge concern. The more people became wealthy with material things, they more they lacked spiritual and social enrichment.

Even if blacks are having difficulty being together with their family members in America, they should not think that they are an isolated case. Racism and segregation happen all around the world. Non-equality between whites and blacks is not the only issue that they need to resolve. They also need to move the world to become tolerant of each other regardless of race.

Nevertheless, one cannot ignore that the surge of the Negroes in the United States was remarkable. They were more passionate and dedicated when it came to fighting for equality. And it would be sad if the blacks would fail in their movement toward equality.

Aside from taking action, it is crucial for everyone involved to be attentive to what is going on in the social climate of the country and the world — blacks are no exception. It is important for everyone to know the progress of social changes. If they don't, all will suffer and perish.

—O—

Of course, racism is not just an American issue; it happens all over the world. Neocolonialism greatly exacerbated it. To make matters worse, religion, especially Christianity, enforced the other problems in the world house.

Racism and materialism are two things that can shake and ruin the foundation of the world house. On the flip side, poverty also creates cracks on the foundation. And with the accelerating growth of the world's population, poverty will be further amplified.

Materialism and racism are things that cannot be immediately resolved. But poverty is. The people within the world house must work together to fight poverty and reinforce the foundation. All people are interdependent after all.

Another problem in the world house is war. Large countries

talk about peace but focus on creating defenses and improving their military power. It is important that they focus on resolving issues through nonviolent means. It worked on a smaller scale, so why would it not work on the big picture?

—O—

Countries should be person-oriented instead of material-oriented. Even if everyone focuses on scientific evolutions, they should also be aware of freedom revolutions. They must be conscious of how damaging and damning militarism, materialism, and racism are.

They must get past capitalism and communism. They must know the truth and the significance of both individualism and collectivism. The changes have started. Soviet Union, for example, has moved away from its traditional communist roots. It is now edging toward individualism and collectivism.

The world needs a revolution of values to make people realize the fairness and justification of new and old policies. It will also make citizens be more mindful of poverty and wealth.

America needs to lead this revolution. It has the resources and manpower to accomplish it. There is no reason why it cannot start providing decent salaries to public servants such as teachers and social workers. And there is no reason why it shouldn't balance out the salaries of physical labor-based workers like housecleaners, laundry workers, and day laborers.

This is an effective solution to defeating communism. Instead of waging wars, simply improving the people's quality of life will be enough for them to stop considering communism. With that said, it does not mean that the United States should focus on being anti-communism. It must present itself and its action as progressing democracy to the next level.

America does not fear communism. It is fear that fuels the gears of war. Remember that communism is the byproduct of democracy. A nation with a failed democracy often turns to communism — or worse, anarchy.

All over the world, people are constantly battling oppression and exploitation. The people of the world house have started rebelling against the old thinking and unfair systems. The ones who have experienced suffering are always the one who can see a brighter light.

The world needs a revolution of values to preserve individual societies. To do that, mankind must be loyal to mankind. Each nation should help and uplift one another. And there is no better time to start than now. Procrastinating or ignoring these will only spell doom for the world. It might not be now, but it might be tomorrow.

Appendix: Programs and Prospects

Education

The good thing about the United States is that it is focused on education. Naturally, the goal is to educate children and allow parents to go about their work without worrying about their kids.

Unfortunately for Negroes, schools cannot function the same way. Schools do not assume the responsibility of educating black children. And of course, the poor's children don't have any other choice but to rely on their parents for education.

This is another social divide that hinders the development and prosperity of the Negroes and the poor. With this disadvantage comes the prejudice toward Negro parents. People say that blacks are irresponsible when it comes to rearing educated citizens.

It is true that family should play a significant role in educating the children. However, they shouldn't be burdened with the task of doing everything. Letting a child get left behind just because he or she is a child of black parents is unjustifiable. Educators should see past colors and be dedicated to developing the future of children regardless of ethnicity and race.

Employment

A developing economy will not guarantee the employment security of Negroes. It does improve the quality of life of citizens, but it must not end there.

Currently, the Negro youth is having a more difficult time obtaining employment. They live as if they are in the middle of an economic crisis. They live as if they are not citizens of the country.

This situation came about because of how the educational system treats young Negroes. Employment opportunities require educational credential and certificates, which the Negro youth does not have. This effectively prevents any black youth from getting jobs from the government and private sectors.

To resolve this, employers must adhere to the "Jobs First, Training Later" employment model. With the current system of education and existing job policies, everything happens in reverse. And this always leads to people being trained for nonexistent jobs or jobs that they will not actually get.

Because training has been mandated to come first, employers are able to avoid issues. The employer does not need to adjust to potential recruits. If the applicant does not have the required knowledge and skills, they are not considered for the job. This basically limits the list of jobs of Negro youth who do not have a broad educational background.

The government must work with and incentivize the private sector for providing on-the-job training instead of expecting applicants to be already trained. If the private sector believes that they would be at risk of getting untrainable employees, the government should cover the costs for resources used on such people.

Rights

The rich often have the power over the poor, and they often have the advantage of being fully protected by the law. They have the resources to deal with court orders, and they can benefit from any loophole.

The poor, on the other hand, do not have any form of power. They have little or limited means to defend themselves on a court trial. And more often than not, they do not even know their rights, much less the rules and regulations to safeguard those rights.

This is a huge concern when it comes to the distribution of political power. The poor do not know the extent of the benefits they can get from welfare.

APPENDIX

Housing

The United States has been failing to improve its housing industry. Building a house can cost a lot, and it is getting pricier every year. In fact, the cost of housing increases faster than those of other items. Despite the advances in construction, the industry fails to implement and apply new measures.

The state of housing employment in the country is almost only accessible by whites and blacks are often denied. The steps to gain employment in the housing industry are too complicated. The result is a more divisive America: suburbs are generally white territory, while blacks dominate the cities.

Despite the movement making positive changes to eradicate segregation and racism, the government is still, in effect, leading the country to continual segregation. This also makes it difficult for people to have easy access to better living conditions, transportation, employment, and education.

Conclusion

The people that joined the movement deserve to be honored for fighting against the system together with King. As mentioned, even though King did have some mishaps that Coretta Scott King had come to terms with, there is no doubt that his life's work is deserving of praise.

It is truly wonderful how a simple question like asking where you are in your life or in society can let you experience catharsis. Knowing yourself and your role in society can lead you to think of what you can do for the community. The people that joined the movement definitely found the answer to that question, and it allowed them to move to a place where they were truly needed.

It is refreshing to be with other people fighting for the same thing. Your voice will be heard. Your angst and repressed feelings will be freed.

Despite the negativity that surrounded the movement, King and his close allies were able to control and maintain their crowd. They were able to remind them what they were fighting for and what they were up against. Remembering their goal has kept them focused.

CONCLUSION

It is no wonder that King had the heart of a 60-year-old despite being only 39 when he died. It is true — doctors discovered this while conducting an autopsy of his body. King was so dedicated to the cause that his heart aged rapidly.

Being a black man in the 1950s and 1960s was hard enough, but being labeled as aggressive and hateful can make life outside the ghetto suffocating. That was the backlash of the movement. It is true that the demonstrations garnered supporters, but after people received news that a minority in the movement had violent tendencies, supporters dwindled and those who were opposed only became even more scornful of blacks.

Putting oneself in a black person's shoes during that time can be difficult. The degree of discrimination they faced was truly terrifying. And the most frightening part of it all was that even if people were directly providing bad judgment against you, they would still claim that they are not racist or discriminating. That behavior is evident even today.

For example, despite all the slurs and bad attitude toward people of color, President Donald J. Trump will still insist that he is the least racist person you will ever meet. In one sense, he is actually better than the white folks of yore. At the very least, he is willing to take black or other ethnic minority as employees — whereas back then, it would take a miracle for a black to get a job or even be allowed to patronize a business.

On the other hand, the church and religion have been some of the most discriminating agencies — even today. Since slavery is now considered "bad" by the church, they need to look for other people to discriminate: gays and lesbians. And that is just Christianity alone. Think about Islam for a moment and imagine how Muslims would react toward the LGBTQ community.

The Southern Baptists discriminate the LGBTQ community by simply shunning them. The government and religious sectors in some Middle Eastern countries discriminate the LGBTQ community by persecuting them, often to the point of killing them.

Just like the black movement, the LGBTQ community is fighting to be considered "human beings," too. For the past few years, the community has been lobbying to legalize gay marriage. And just like the blacks, they are met with resistance. A state even approved gay marriage, but people in power still do not like the idea — to the point that a bill giving bakers the right to deny gay couples wedding cakes has been passed into legislation.

Thankfully, the LGBTQ is a strong community — not to mention that they were not subjected to cruel treatment (a.k.a slavery) like the blacks. They did not need to cope by drinking or drugging themselves. After all, they are still as free as any other regular citizen in the United States. If the state they reside in does not accept them for who they are, they can just move to another. For the most part, they are not being segregated or denied employment because of their sexual orientation.

Now that King is gone and the movement ended decades ago, where are we going now? First, even if the movement is over, the fight is not. As long as poverty and discrimination are rampant in the country, Americans should continue the fight.

People must become more active in fighting poverty and eliminating racism. Americans must always be vigilant about what the government is doing. They must always remind the people who have gained power in politics that they have the responsibility of taking care of all the citizens, regardless of status, race, and gender.

People should follow the solutions and suggestions that King shared in his book. They will greatly help in repeating the positive side of history. People should not let go of hope; they need to act on starting nonviolent protesting, and continue doing so until the ideal equality is achieved.

People all over the world should start building the world house. They must make sure that its foundation is solid and not marred by materialism. Everyone has the moral responsibility of defending and protecting those in pain, of calling out unfair and unjust governing, of embracing diversity.

The wealthy nations of the world should continue working to abolish poverty at a global scale. Countries like the United States have already improved its discrimination and segregation issues — even though President Trump is still attempting to isolate the United States from the rest of the world by building border walls and drastically changing immigration laws.

On the individual level, again, it cannot be stressed that everyone must stay away from materialism. When you are on your last days, the things that would matter to you would be your experiences and not your wealth. So, as long as you are still able, you must help in resolving social concerns and encouraging freedom revolutions.

Final Thoughts

Hey! Did you enjoy this book? We sincerely hope you thoroughly enjoyed this short read and have gotten immensely valuable insights that will help you in any areas of your life.

Would it be too greedy if we ask for a review from you?

It takes 1 minute to leave 1 review to possibly influence 1 more person's decision to read just 1 book which may change their 1 life. Your 1 minute matters and we value it and thank you so much for giving us your 1 minute. If it sucks, just say it sucks. Period.

FREE BONUS

P.S. Is it okay if we overdeliver?

Here at Abbey Beathan Publishing, we believe in overdelivering way beyond our reader's expectations. Is it okay if we overdeliver?

Here's the deal, we're going to give you an extremely valuable cheatsheet of "Accelerated Learning". We've partnered up with Ikigai Publishing to present to you the exclusive bonus of "Accelerated Learning Cheatsheet"

What's the catch? We need to trust you… You see, we want to overdeliver and in order for us to do that, we've to trust our reader to keep this bonus a secret to themselves. Why? Because we don't want people to be getting our exclusive accelerated learning cheatsheet without even buying our books itself. Unethical, right?

Ok. Are you ready?

Simply Visit this link: http://bit.ly/acceleratedcheatsheet

We hope you'll enjoy our free bonuses as much as we've enjoyed preparing it for you!

Free Bonus #2: Free Book Preview of Summary: Dreams from my Father

The Book at a Glance

Chapter 1 is all about Barack Obama's origins. He was born to a white mother and a black African father. His grandparents were witness to racial discrimination in the past, and their being liberal-minded and how they respected "colored" people led to his parents union. Although Barack's father left them when he was only 2 years old, his mother and grandparents never spoke ill of him. They still remembered and shared their memories of him as a dignified, intelligent, and graceful gentleman.

Chapter 2 talks about how Barack immigrated to Indonesia when his mother married an Indonesian. In the new country, he turned to his stepfather Lolo for guidance and advice. He learned how to survive, and learned life-long values such as honesty, fairness, and being straightforward. He was also exposed to the cruel world of poverty and violence.

Chapter 3 brings him back to America, where he was required to go to school. His mother stayed in Indonesia with Lolo and his new sister, Maya. She would later join him in America. He would also meet his father for the first time since he left. He would live with him for a month and get to know the father that he never knew.

Chapter 4 shares how Barack went through high school and his experiences living with his grandparents. In fact, he had an eye-opening experience when his grandmother was harassed by a black man on the way to work. As a result, he turned to books trying to search for answers to his identity and on the roots of racism.

In chapter 5, Barack, having found his voice, became active in school rallies. During this time, his mother talked him into building a future by starting college. He would turn to one of his gramps' friends, Frank the poet, and would be warned to keep his eyes open. It was a difficult time, and he further experienced an identity crisis.

In chapter 6, Barack takes the opportunity of a transfer program to Columbia University and transfers to Manhattan. He stays with a Pakistani friend who was an illegal immigrant and became serious about his studies. During the summer, when his mother visited him with Maya, his sister, he would learn of the true story behind his parents' separation and would serve as a realization. He would carry his father's memories even after his death and find a new identity for himself in light of his father.

Chapter 7 talks about how Barack was inspired to become an organizer. He was promoted as a financial writer but later resigned his post. At first, his dreams of becoming an organizer slipped away, if not for his half-sister's phone call that gave him a push. He got hired by a Jewish organizer, Marty Kaufman, and set off to Chicago.

Chapter 8 shows Barack's first few days as an organizer in Chicago. He attended the CCRC rally, which composed of people who were laid off from work. The first few days were full of challenges as there was trouble talking to people and coming up with an issue that everyone believed was worth fighting for.

In chapter 10, Barack was almost ready to give up. However, his and his co-organizers realizations motivated him to do better and make a difference. In the end, he was successful in organizing a meeting with the Mayor's Office Employment and Training (MET), and the result was a promise to have a MET intake center within the vicinity in six months' time.

Chapter 10 speaks of winter, which was a time of realization for Barack. From the stories he heard from the organization leaders, he realized that they were fighting for a cause due to their past – just like him. This led him to open up and relate better to others.

Barack finally meets his half-sister from Kenya, named Auma, in chapter 11. During her visit, she told him things about their father, which made him get to know him from another's point of view. It was in this reunion with her sister that he finally felt free from the memories of his father.

Chapter 12 talks about the success Barack was finally making as an organizer. He eventually separated ways with this boss, Marty. They were able to launch the new MET intake center in Roseland, and also get some young parents involved in fighting for health causes.

In chapter 13, Barack employed a recruit named Johnnie, whom he got along well. He also visited his half-brother in Washington, D.C., and learned more from him. However, Roy's attitude towards their father was more of bitterness.

Chapter 14 talks about how Barack decided to pursue law at Harvard and selected Johnnie to replace him as lead organizer. Their current project was to target the public schools with the help of religious congregations. Barack attended his first ever service and was moved to tears with the realization of hope.

Chapter 15 brings Barack to Kenya, where he meets British men on the plane who were to make up for the "lack of trained professionals" in Kenya. He managed to have his luggage accidentally sent to Johannesburg, and was helped by a lovely stewardess who knew his father. He felt a sense of belonging in Kenya, but the locals still saw him as American.

In chapter 16, Barack meets his other relatives and learns of the rift among his two aunts, Zeituni and Sarah, due to his father's inheritance. He also meets with his half-brother, seventeen-year-old Bernard. Later on, he would meet his father's other wife, Ruth, and his stepbrother Mark, who also studies in America.

Chapter 17 is a family reunion, when Roy comes home to Kenya earlier than expected. Barack and Auma had just come back from a safari, and he was enjoying the last few days of his vacation.

Chapter 18 introduces more of Barack's extended family. He met his grandmother, two uncles, and his grandfather's brother. He also noticed that people would always ask him for something when he arrived. His relatives highly regarded him due to his father's stories about him.

In chapter 19, Barack learns more about his grandfather's discipline and how he prospered due to hard work, about his father's diligence to study abroad, and about the events that happened to his father. He finally understood and felt complete.

The epilogue fast-forwards to the future. Barack pursued law and gave back to the community by helping out community organizers and churches. He met his future wife, Michelle, who was immediately loved by his family. They got married despite some deaths in both their families.

Part 1: Origins

Chapter 1

Barack Obama was named after his father, who was an African Kenyan and a member of the Luo tribe. His father was a smart man who won a scholarship in Nairobi and was among the chosen few who attended university in the United States. He was the first African student at the University of Hawaii, where he graduated at the top of his class, and became president of the International Students Association. He also met his future wife in Hawaii. However, he was asked to go back to Africa for his duties. His son, Barack or Barry, was only two years old at that time. Mother and son remained in the United States.

Barack Junior's mother and grandparents talked fondly of his father. His grandparents told him of a story wherein a white man at the bar was being racist and tried to humiliate his father. His father lectured the man. As a result, the man tried to buy his forgiveness. When Barack was 21, his aunt Jane, who had been a stranger until then, called from Nairobi. She announced that his father had died in a car crash.

One of the things that Barack wondered about was why his mother's parents permitted her to marry his father. Barack's mother was white, and his father was African and black. Eventually, he learned that his grandparents were raised in decent and respectable families, so discrimination was not known. His grandparents also told stories about their past, which were filled with romance, drama, and action. In fact, the stories were always interesting. He also learned that his grandparents eloped just before the Pearl Harbor bombing and that his grandfather enlisted in the army.

His grandfather was also the adventurous type who loved to venture on new starts. He was also poetic and a freethinker. This liberal-mindedness paved the way for his father's invitation to dinner. When Barack's mother invited his father for dinner, his grandfather was struck by his resemblance to his favorite singer, Nat King Cole. When dinner ended, his grandparents commented how dignified, intelligent, and graceful he was – and he also loved his British accent.

When the family moved to Texas, they had their experiences with racial discrimination. These incidents explained why his grandparents allowed his white mother to marry a black man. First was when his grandmother, called Toot or Tutu, spoke with a World War II veteran who was black. She addressed him as Mr. Reed and found him to be very dignified. However, she was called out by the secretary that black men should never be addressed as "Mister". She continued calling him Mr. Reed, but the janitor kept his distance.

Another instance was when his mother came home one day from school and befriended a black girl. The other students threw stones at them and called his mother a "nigger lover". The next day, Barack's grandfather took a leave from work, spoke to the principal, and reported the students who had thrown stones. The principal responded that white girls should not play with colored races.

Eventually, Barack's mother and father were married by a justice of the peace in a quiet ceremony; then, they moved to Hawaii. In Hawaii, there were many different cultures such as Japanese, Chinese, and Filipino. Racism was a thing of the past in Hawaii, and here is where the family became comfortable.

However, Barack still wondered why his father left. His mother and grandparents painted a picture of how amazing he was, but he still did not understand. He even found articles about his father and a photograph of him. Barack felt that something was amiss in his childhood and he grew older, not knowing his father.

Read More...

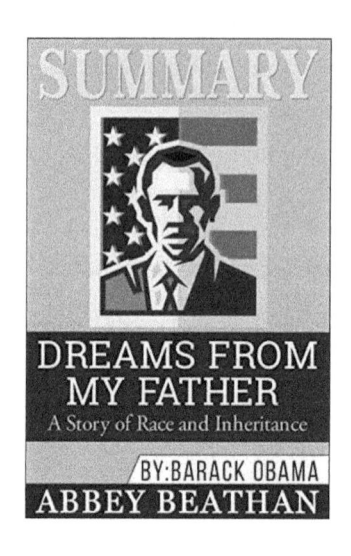

CPSIA information can be obtained
at www.ICGtesting.com
Printed in the USA
BVHW081935270819
556932BV00001B/309/P